72 GENDERS

DEFINING GENDER IDENTITIES

DAYAA HAWKINS

72 Genders – Defining Gender Identities
by
Dayaa Hawkins

The proposal that there are 72 genders is both unfortunate and laughable. Much of this disinformation has been unintentionally propagated via Joe Rogan's podcast, as he has interviewed various academics who have misled Joe on the topic. But the true culprit where the figure originates is Facebook's convoluted attempt to include any and all gender references to their Gender options list. Fifty of these were initially added by Facebook, then an additional twenty one were added by Facebook's UK site.

It is Facebook's failure to actually research all the terms and remove redundant or unnecessary entries which has caused this setback in the advancement of equal rights, and in all probability has added to the animosity some bear towards the LGBTQ community.

Here are all the genders as erroneously presented by Facebook.

Facebook 50

Agender
Androgyne
Androgynes
Androgynous
Bigender

Cis, Cis Female, Cis Male, Cis Man, Cis Woman
Cisgender, Cis gender Female, Cisgender Male,
Cisgender Man, Cisgender Woman

Female to Male
FTM
Gender Fluid
Gender Nonconforming
Gender Questioning
Gender Variant
Genderqueer

Intersex

Male to Female
MTF
Neither
Neutrois
Non-binary
Other
Pangender

Trans
Trans Female
Trans Male
Trans Man
Trans Person
Trans*Female
Trans*Male
Trans*Man
Trans*Person
Trans*Woman

Transexual
Transexual Female
Transexual Male
Transexual Man
Transexual Person
Transexual Woman
Transgender Female
Transgender Person
Transmasculine

Two-spirit

UK Facebook 21 additions

Asexual
Female to male trans man
Female to male transgender man
Female to male transexual man
F2M

Gender neutral
hermaphrodite

Intersex man
Intersex person
Intersex woman

Male to female trans woman
Male to female transgender woman
Male to female transsexual woman
Man
M2F

Polygender – normally give to those with four or more
T*man
T*woman
Two* person
Two-spirit person
Woman

I will now define all the various gender terms, then correct and/or omit the list.

Agender – identifies as neither male nor female

Androgynous – the combination of masculine and feminine characteristics. The use of androgyne and androgynes is both redundant and unnecessary.

Bigender – identifies as two genders

Cisgender – often abbreviated as cis, is the term for people whose gender identity matches the sex they were born with. These additions are all the same – six of one, half a dozen of another. The traditional male or female gender choices can be used. It is really just a way for those who do not identify as either male or female to separate themselves from the rest of "normal" society, however they may seek to define it as such.

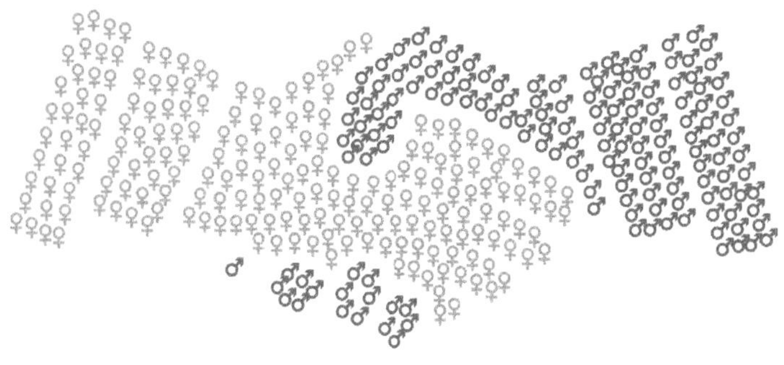

Female to Male (FTM) – a person who was born female but identifies as male. It is not its own gender, but a subcategory of transgender. As Dalmatians are a type of Canine, FTM is a type of transgender.

Genderfluid – a gender identity which varies over time. How one identifies can change every day or even every few hours. No. Genderfluid is not real. You may have a hormonal, chemical, or psychological imbalance which effects your sense of perception, but variable gender identity from moment to moment is not a classification of gender.

Gender Nonconforming – refers to people who do not adhere to society's rules about dress and activities for people that are based on their biological sex and gender assignment. Since gender conformity is a social construct, this is not an actual type of gender.

Gender Questioning – an exploration and self-defining of one's own gender – not an actual gender.

Gender Variant – same as Gender Nonconforming, thus redundant and unnecessary.

Genderqueer – also known as non-binary, is a catch-all category for gender identities that are not exclusively male or female.

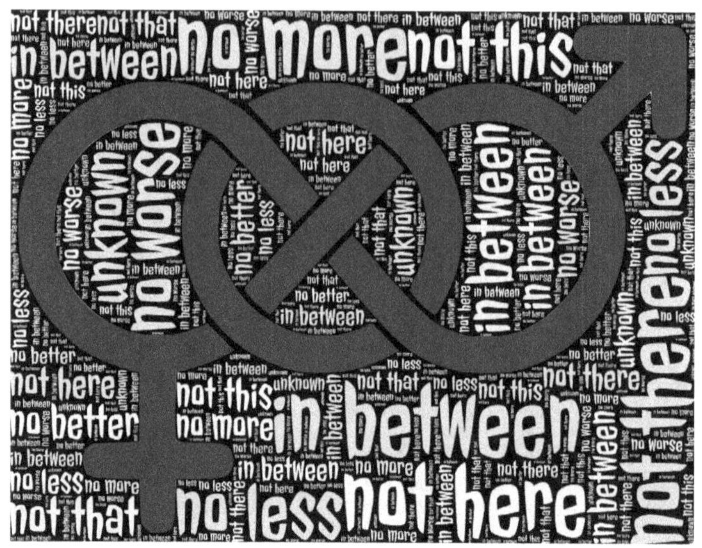

Intersex – people who are born with any of several variations in sex characteristics including, chromosomes, gonads, sex hormones, or genitals, that, according to the UN Office of the High Commissioner for Human Rights, "do not fit the typical definitions for male or female bodies." Thus, people with actual, physical abnormalities, not psychological crises.

Male to Female (MTF) – a person who was born male but identifies as a female. It is not its own gender, but a subcategory of transgender.

Neither – another of the several redundant classifications used by Facebook, such as agender, non-binary, or neutrois, which all mean neither, anyway.

Neutrois – a non-binary gender identity which is often associated with a "neutral" or "null" gender.

Non-binary – a gender identity which does not fit the male and female binary.

Other – do I really need to explain this one to you?

Pangender – a person whose gender identity is not limited to one gender and who may feel like a member of all genders at the same time. Again, no. Like genderfluid, this is not a real gender identity. A large portion of human society is afflicted by the need to stand out, to separate themselves from others, to make themselves feel special or important; this stems from the fact that they are neither special nor important.

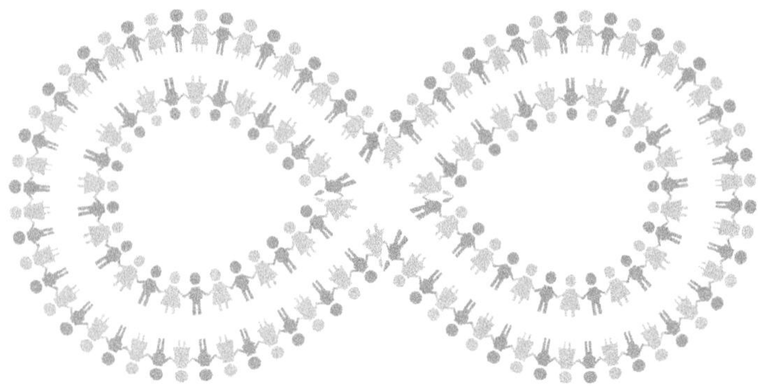

Transgender – people who have a gender identity that differs from their sex at birth. This is the only choice you need, all others Facebook uses are redundant terms for transgender, or are subcategories of transgender and thus are not their own independent gender classification. Remember my dog analogy?

Two-Spirit – a gender identity of certain Indigenous North American peoples. Basically, a racial-specific transgender person; thus not an actual gender, but once again a subcategory of transgender.

UK Facebook 21 additions

Asexuality – the lack of sexual attraction to others. This is a sexual preference, even if that preference is no sex at all. It is not a gender classification. I will address this issue later in the book.

Gender Neutral – just the British version of Neither. See the previous definition of Neither listed earlier.

Hermaphrodite – a person in which reproductive organs of both sexes are present. It is surprising that Facebook did not originally include this as an option. Though it would fall under the Intersex category. See! Facebook does know what subcategories are, they just choose not to use them.

Polygender – a person who has multiple genders; normally given to those with four or more. This is the exact same as pangender, and just like it, is not a real gender.

All the 17 other UK Facebook additions are just unnecessary subcategories of Intersex or Transgender. It's sad that the British can't even understand English.

The use of an asterisk is meant to refer to any sex or gender identities that use the trans prefix. So the asterisk is used incorrectly (trans*) instead of a simple dash (trans-). And in some cases has been abbreviated further to just T*. Once again, just another way for people to try and feel special. Poor things.

Tumblr Genders or Get The Fuck Out Of Here

In researching gender identities online, you may run into a major roadblock that has corrupted all search engines – the dipshits on Tumblr. These idiots have falsely created **hundreds** of genders, NONE of which are real genders. The master list they have created is mindnumbingly ignorant, and more than a little insulting to those who experience real gender-related issues.

Here are a few of the gems:

Astralgender – a gender that feels connected to space
Cadensgender – a gender that's easily influenced by music
Dragonkin – identify as dragons
Existigender – a gender which only exists or is noticeable when thought about or when conscious effort is made to notice it
Foggender – a gender which is close to a certain gender, but cannot be directly pinpointed due to brainfog (a lack of concentration or wakefulness associated with ADHD, fibromyalgia, depression, etc)
Frostgender – a gender that feels cold and snowy
Genderfuzz – having multiple genders that are blurred together, making each one indistinguishable from the others
Nyctogender – a gender consisting of darkness or related to it
Otherkin – identify as not fully human
Witchgender – a gender that has closeness or connection to witchcraft or magic

Now we can quickly cover the fabricated sexual orientations since asexuality was erroneously included as a gender.

Asexuality in the modern context is the lack of sexual attraction to others. Though nonsexual would be a better term as the standard definition of asexual means having no sexual organs or reproduction independent of sexual processes.

No, it is not a sexual orientation, merely a condition of lack of sexual desire. This can be caused by low self-esteem, depression, anxiety, social stigma, religious extremism, or various forms of abuse. And it is most certainly not a gender or subcategory of gender.

Ace is an umbrella term which includes demisexual, semisexual, asexual-ish, and sexual-ish. Idiot is another umbrella term which includes demisexual, semisexual, asexual-ish, and sexual-ish.

Demisexual is a person who does not experience sexual attraction unless they form an emotional connection. The term demisexual is intended to designate being "halfway between" sexual and asexual, but this is an improper use of the prefix demi- which means half or lesser.

Gray Asexuality (also Gray Sexuality, Gray-A, Grace, or Gray Ace) – is the spectrum between asexuality and sexuality. No. It is not a spectrum. Have sex with whoever you want. Stop complicating sexuality and making up nonsense to feel better about yourself.

Semisexual – a person who feels sexual attraction but has no desire to act on it.

None of these are real sexual orientations or gender identities, they are preferences; your feelings and opinions about sex.

They are all nonsense words made up by people with a poor grasp of the English language and do not know the meaning of sexual orientation. And who are having a hard time coming to grips with the probability that they are unfuckable.

There are many people misusing terms or trying to make new ones and in the process are confusing sex, gender, sexual orientation, and gender identity. Not to mention the horrendous inaccuracies generated by Reddit, Tumblr, Urban Dictionary, and the rest of the misguided internet.

They tried with womyn and womon in the 1970's, and that didn't work out. You're sure not going to convince 320 million people is the US to learn a new pronoun language because you are uncomfortable with your own identity. That is your issue to work out, not ours. You might pull it off in some of the extremely liberal colleges which exist in their own bubble, and maybe Canada, but it's not going to apply in the real world. And for a final dose of painful honesty – no one cares. Your personal identity, your hangups, your foibles, your hopes, your dreams, your desires – no one cares. It is a big, lonely, uncaring world. You and your problems are the least of society's concerns.

Don't let uptight, rightwing assholes like Jordan Peterson define you. But don't let people like Sam Killermann define you, either. You are not just a checkbox on his gender fluid accounting spreadsheet. You define you. You be you.

BE
YOUR
OWN
FLOWER

Maybe genderflora *is* the way to go. I like flowers. What? You got a problem with daffodils, mother fucker?

Be your own flower.

Just. . . be.

US: 877-565-8860 / Canada: 877-330-6366

Need to talk? Call Trans Lifeline! Their peer support hotline is run by and for trans people. They're available 7am-1am PST / 9am-3am CST / 10a-4am EST. Volunteers may be available during off hours.

Online at: translifeline.org

Dayaa Hawkins, child of immigrants, is a proud Indo-American and grew up in Castillo de Roca, NM. She attended UCDR and received an agBS in Psychology with an emphasis on Human Sexuality. She enjoys hiking, dancing, laughing, and searching for lost cities beneath the sands of the New Mexico desert.